For my grandchildren Gabrielle, Andrea Rose, Asher, and Elan—
this, too, their inheritance.

*There are only two lasting bequests we can hope to give our children.
One of them is roots, the other wings.*

—Johann Wolfgang von Goethe

*How sad and bad and mad it was—
But then how it was sweet!*

—Robert Browning

Contents

from
AN OUTWARD TRACK

from
NAMING THE DARKNESS

from
IN THE SHADOW OF PARADISE

UNCOLLECTED POEMS

Foreword

Each of Jane Ellen Glasser's words sounds like it's found a home, often with a brilliant and surprising fit. I think of Millay who loved to astonish with God-granted word choices as well as content. Glasser's mind has something like a skill-set composed of poetry principles and blazing insights that she uses to photograph everything she sees, senses, thinks, feels. Click, click. There's a poem, sometimes of complex depths and sometimes profoundly simple. One of my favorite poems comes from her absorption with birds, "How to Make Friends with Wild Ducks."

> If you come often enough
> to that place
> where the earth hugs
> a pond's perimeter
> and keep your distance,
> eventually you will become
> part of the landscape.
>
> If you come often enough
> and sit statue-still,
> content to be
> an observing eye,
> the space between you
> will shrink.
>
> If you come often enough
> and bring treats,
> they will come,
> a waddling raft,
> to greet you.
>
> If you come often enough,
> on a day
> when you do not come
> they will keep
> listening for your footsteps.
>
> Sometimes this even works with humans.

Can there be a better way of describing a bunch of ducks coming toward you than as "a waddling raft," or can a poem have a more startling but obvious conclusion? There is a fetish for quiet, and an almost total lack of assertiveness in the call for ducks, made more compelling by the hidden enchantment of the repeated word "come." Such moments of grace are always on the way with Glasser.

I've been reading Glasser's books or listening to Glasser at readings while holding my breath for forty years now (we once shared a publisher), from her first book to this one, her sixth, and have never been disappointed. She is, in fact, one of the finest poets in America, but still underrated and almost unclassifiable. If pushed, I would say she's a postmodernist, like most of the rest of us raised in postmodern air. She has gone beyond modernism because the camera in her mind has set beyond traditional forms and become postmodern in that she uses objective reality to take off for subjective ones in which she finds new rules and revelations.

Her poems, regardless of eventual flights, usually spring from the ordinary (an electric blanket, hearing aids, spring cleaning, etc.) but are, nevertheless, worlds of their own, attending to their problems and fashions, for the most part oblivious to such distractions as politics, finance, war, organized religions. The book is an autobiography in poetry, ruled by imagery that speaks of her loves, losses, experiences in nature, and fields of emotion in relentless but soft metaphor and often humor. Sometimes, she only alludes to or suggests an event, making the event's aftermath, rather than the event itself, the cogent thing—as if the interpretations, usually made alone, were the poetic payoff, filled with useful secrets and magical properties.

In "Cracks," the event is her noticing cracks on Mona's Lisa's lips, how "In Rilke's elegy/ death zigzags/ on a china cup." Then springs her subjective universe, didactic bent, gift of phrase, metaphor, and, lastly, metaphor mixed with ecclesiastical profundity.

Don't give me
perfection
immune to cracks.

Don't give me
the unbroken,
the safely stored
in airless faults.

Every scar
is the short hand
of an important story.

Each crack
is a door opening
onto a larger room.

Most often, she does the opposite by telling a story or at length elaborately setting the stage, then knocking us out with a conclusion by metaphor to the heart that elucidates the truths of our living.

Like footprints sucked from a rug,
a profound loneliness
haunts the immaculate
rooms of my house.

("Spring Cleaning")

Sometimes, Glasser's imagery is so strikingly beautiful it almost takes leave of sense and takes over the whole poem from the start. Such a magical bouquet of non-sense lifts into the wind and treetops, arriving into poetry as flower ("Japanese Cherry Blossom") and ending with one of the most effective groups of lines in all her work.

....the wind will begin its scattering work
and it will rain pink petals for a week.
As reverie follows bliss, green will follow pink.
And green can live for months on memory.

In her desire to present new realities, Glasser sometimes empathizes with such things as bats, rivers, concepts, rocks, and rain, and she lets them speak, feel, listen, and offer lessons, albeit unconsciously. She writes a love letter to the rain and lets its mood spill into hers after it tap-dances on her roof and causes the sky to spasm. In "Rumination on Romantic Love," "Romance refuses to sleep/ its life away in the same bed." A June bird ("June Birds") flies into its reflection and shows her what love is like when it crashes and dies. In "Soloist," a dove sings a five-note aria and teaches her how to write a poem.

...this is the way
a poem writes itself,
note by solitary note
on the prevailing air.

For Glasser, in every cold river there's a baptism, in every leaved tree multiple parables, exempla, fables, metaphors that push us to epiphanies that are decked out with imagery. Her poems capture her life at every turn and twist, at each period or moment of joy, boredom, or sorrow.

Glasser's fascination with poetry as an outlet for exploring and making sense of her feelings began as an adolescent, and the family's move to Greenwich Village when she was a high school student served as an important source of inspiration. Attracted to the "Bohemian life," she haunted bookstores and cafes, reading everything she could get her hands on. Later, when she attended Old Dominion University to earn her Master of Humanities degree, she was blessed with "a lifetime opportunity"—the University's hiring of Pulitzer Prize winner W. D. Snodgrass as visiting writer. In lieu of a traditional thesis, she was granted permission to study under Snodgrass to produce her first book of poetry, "An Outward Track." Although considered the father of confessional poetry, ironically Snodgrass steered her away from poets like Anne Sexton and Sylvia Plath, deepening her appreciation for poets like Rilke, Jarrell, and Frost.

During the depths of marital difficulties and later divorce, she had to go no further for inspiration than the backyard of her home, situated on a cove of the Lafayette River. At the time, I remember being so obsessed with one of her verses that I used to mutter it to myself when I had troubles with women, finances, cars, etc.

> Stronger than my need to keep things full,
> the river has its own and deeper pull.
> Twice each day it makes an outward track.
> Unlike most human things, it twice comes back.
>
> ("The River")

Rivers can be depended on; men not so much. She turns confessional.

> You turn away in dreams.
> The wind whines through the night
> like a lonely heroine.
> I cannot set you right.
>
> ("The Blanket")

> "Nothing is perfect," you said, settling
> in a soft chair. The story I had been
> telling myself about where we would go
> from here evaporated like a whisper.

...
where could we go from here now
that we know what we know.

("Existential Questions")

As my old discoverer, the late poet, James Whitehead, famously wrote: "The end of style for honest men is clarity." Glasser is always crystal clear. Her poems draw you in and make you understand. Unlike the efforts of some of her postmodern brothers and sisters, they don't utilize the necessary obscurity that keeps some decipherers in universities employed and honored. Among the techniques of postmodernists and some modernists, she mostly avoids self-reference, deliberate obscurity, unreliable narrators, irony, fragmentation, satire, shades of grey, hostile attacks on the objective, and projective verse, though she would accept Olson's notion that form is an extension of content. A former high-school English teacher, she obeys the laws of the sentence, every wish of punctuation and grammar.

Glasser is very much a presence in her poems, if not self-referential. Odd, then, that she withdraws (seemingly) the most when she writes of a daughter's death by automobile accident when driving home from her college graduation; she knows that her withdrawal leaves an emotional vacuum the reader rushes in to fill. Below are two remarkable poems.

—Planted in memory of my daughter Jessica

This third spring, a blush,
barely a tinge of pink,
poked from a thin branch.

I have known them
wild in the mountains,
the first splashes of color
in the blue woods.

Again this summer
the few leaves, bitten
by blight, singed by sun,
hang like sick hearts.

("Red Bud")

There were two of them
as if what they carried
was too heavy for one.

They stood in the doorway,
dark blue uniforms
backed in light.

Their faces were not sad or happy.

They asked to come in
They had something to tell her.

Was she alone?
Was there anyone they could call
to be with her?

They told her to sit down.

Together they pulled
from their mouths
the name of her daughter.

Together they placed
the unbearable weight
in her lap.

("The Visit")

Although Glasser's poems do not shy away from pain, the titles of her books (from *Naming the Darkness* to *Light Persists*) indicate that, over the years, her poems have taken on acceptance, even gratitude, exemplified in these excerpts.

I will wear gratitude like a red coat,
forbearing the shifting
seasons of hope and doubt.

("Vows for the New Year")

I found myself—
a woman/ alone
on a mountain top
dancing naked

beneath the tipped
smile of a moon
and the winking stars.

("A Brief History")

Say I was perfectly flawed.
Say I was human.

("Last Wishes")

In this mode, the poet tells us to shed illusions, be thankful for lessons learned, and appreciate continued existence as worthy of celebration.

— Robert P. Arthur

Robert P. Arthur is Writer in low Residence at Wilkes University and author of *Crazy Horse's Woman.*

from
AN OUTWARD TRACK

Old Dominion University, 1980

The Family

Backed in a mottled green
the stilled river
inverts my backyard scene
onto its antiqued mirror.

Across the pictured trees
a fat suburban drake
glides over tarnished leaves
towing his plainer mate.

Out of a child's book
her ducklings straggle straight
behind her. Without a look
she checks her freight;

she keeps them in formation
and knows her place.
Now in a slow motion
of diminishing grace

they paddle downstream
to hold in rougher water
under the male's steam
their ancient order.

Generations in Glass

She looks in, looking for those
she lost. Three faces stare back.
In the mirror of each eye
a miniature floats out.

On the left, a child sings
the stars in and the moon's
white eye. All night the mind
drops crumbs in the dream-wood
only the child can find.

In the vestibule of the ear,
in the labyrinth of sound,
a man waits forever
for the woman on the right eye.
For years he has traveled the blue canal
trying to reach her with his voice.

And now the eyes move back
to see the rest: the little purses
of flesh; the frown that writes
in fine lines. She follows them down
to the lip-pleats, the mouth

where, each morning, a stranger devours
the small bones of her past.

Hard Descents

My father worries about aging. Snow
fell today, a new roof on an old house.
He is greying, inside and out. Hair grows
rings around his forehead. Demons carouse
in those dark caverns. Eyes, moonquakes, unearth
his newsprint dreams. Too old now for spaceflight,
he lands in his soft chair waiting for death's
launching. Outside pupils shrink from daylight,
the glare of snow on bald branches. Forgotten
is the graceful gliding over luscious
ice fields, the risk of imbalance, wanton
legs uplifted. Venture is the slick whim
of youthfulness. Hard descents stay with him.

The Blanket

The wind whips at the window.
I set my dial—a tropic eight.
This dual control, your gift to us.
You like it temperate.

I turn to my poetry; you,
your legal papers, briefs.
After the news one cool leg
trespasses on my zone of sleep.

But I can't sleep. Instead, I take
some hidden novel from the drawer;
Colette, Sagan—no matter—
the plots are similar:

an elegant though aging lady
(her husband out of town)
takes to their bed a lover.
I turn the dial down.

You turn away in dreams.
The wind whines through the night
like a lonely heroine.
I cannot set you right.

The Empty Lot

Beside the house yawns the empty lot
we bought for next to nothing eight years back
if only to improve our looking out;
(it was a dirt-filled dump of weed and rock).

We leveled it with loam and planted seed.
But all that flat, uninterrupted green
was like a thing abandoned when begun—
the underlay of some unfinished scene

that hung in the window of the dining room.
Evenings we would stare out at the grass
as across a table not yet set
and wonder how to fill the emptiness.

One spring we worked the ground beside the marsh.
(Working side by side, we didn't talk.)
From a store of seed, planted in the troughs—
a crop of weeds and one bum row of stalks.

A tennis court, street-side to the east,
gave us something to dream about one June.
By August it was a swimming pool we wanted.
Each season had us sing a different tune.

We even had an architect design,
facing west, a wing across the lot
with walls of glass to reflect the river.
(We put the plans some place we then forgot.)

Except for a neglected jungle gym
and one small pine we planted by the bank
(sad souvenirs of what we planned to do)
eight years later the lot still draws a blank.

Now we never talk about the lot
or look back on what it might have been.
We've gotten used to being next to nothing.
Some empty lots defy a filling in.

Architect of Death

You rake until the blisters formed
then raked them raw. Caught in the motion
as in a trance, you could not stop.
The world divided into green and brown:
the cleared ground of rich Kentucky shag;
the papery shroud of mostly elm and maple
thick enough to turn the grass yellow.
An architect of death, you reached and pulled
to build your monuments of leaf and straw.
You danced like one enchanted or half mad
against the wind that loosened and threw off
leaves onto the place you had cleared.
For the first time in years a rightness
crisped inside your mind. A weightlessness
quickened arms and rake into one
efficient instrument. At five o'clock the sun
singed down; the trees across the river caught.
You had to hurry. You had to finish.
Bags emptied on the gravel street; you must
have bagged a million leaves. Like a boy
with bootlegged matches your eyes flashed
as you ignited pile after pile
until the whole street was bonfire!
For hours you stared at a shadow of ash.

Dream of Devotions

I pray
and you appear.
I think to touch you
and already you are
here touching
as if I were a
sacred braille
or, turning,
a prayer wheel
in your hands.
You breathe into me
as if my flesh could
rise like fresh bread.
I glow and fatten
like a dark berry,
fill and resound
as you pitch and play
a hosanna of breasts,
a hallelujah of thighs.
You wear me
like a necklace
and I sing,
I sing.

We Have to Stop Meeting like This

It is all arranged,
thought through and staged
in advance.
Nothing will be altered.
Nothing will be left to chance.

Wear the clothes that become you:
the jeans ripped at the knee,
the flannel shirt opened to the chest.
You cannot change.
These triangles of flesh
are planned and requisite
to the overall effect.

Don't be nervous.
This tryst is beyond your control, anyway,
and without risk.
Again, I will empty
the back streets and alleys
you must take.
And you will arrive
with synaptic speed
yet smiling and relaxed
as if you had never left.

My need is your key.
Open the door slowly,
as if the air inside
would shatter like glass,
then stand there motionless
for hours
waiting for your cue.

The kiss must be perfect:
tender, yet carnal;
respectful, yet impassioned.
If it's not right at first
we can retake it
again and again.

We have the whole night to practice
and we have been practicing for months.

My husband?
He suspects nothing.
Besides, here in this room,
in this same bed,
he arranges his own affairs around his own dreams.

Don't forget.
Midnight.
The usual place.

Reflection

A mallard, camouflaged in seasonal
umber and emerald, shakes his hackle
at the brown duck trailing him, waddles
to the backdoor for his ritual

day-old bread. My daughter
tosses the stale crusts, the delight of power
contracting in her bird eyes—the dark mirror
of my own dark childhood. I remember

the summers spent in upstate New York
escaping the suffocation of the city, the stark
walls of the room I shared with my sister, the dark
nights my mother said my father had to work.

Mature pines shake their needle fingers
over the Lafayette River; the myrtle's white flowers
yellow like ivory, fall off. My daughter
playing on the edge of the water—

First Snow

It is noon when I wake.
I watch the first snow fall,
surprised to feel surprise.
You kissed me and left
by the backdoor at dawn,
my children safe in their
dreams. I promised to call...

The snow covers and covers.
So suddenly my grounds change.
My daughters spread arms
and legs in the snow; angels
sleep on their white lawn.
Here, and here, a few blades
pierce through like needles.

I promised to call...
but something in me stiffens
and seems, like the trees,
more separate by the shock
of snow. Only yesterday
blackbirds swelled these trees
and connected them with song.

You suspected all along.

Virginia Winters

Sixteen days into another year
and it's warm outside, even for here.
Last fall steals back by red degrees
as if the sun could foliate these trees
or burn the maple by the back door ruddy.
Against the double window of the study,
looking in, a red camellia presses
its eye of sulfur; lost, a cardinal rushes
from September to spurt across this framed,
unsettling scene. These things reclaimed
are like the dreams of winter that, waking, winter
won't remember. Last week I watched these splinter
trees bow with snow. Today they're firewood.
Virginia winters just won't do as they should.

Between Seasons

Even in my dreams the rain
had changed; whispering
through the roof
a conversation.

A man was saying goodbye.

A chill entered the lifting darkness.
The chalk cry of a gull against the sky—

From the back her dress
clung like leaves to her calves.

I pulled the summer
blanket to my chest.

Where he stood
easily waving
the ground was dry
hardening into light.

A Woman

A woman is packing.
Not her own things, these
somehow more familiar.
See how she brings
the faded red sweater
to her nose, fingers
the fur-lined gloves.
She could be a mother
saying a first goodbye...

She has lined the cartons
with tissue sprinkled
with mothballs. Her mind
still turns to preserving.
She smoothes each layer out
like bed linen. Such care
for the move she will
not be making.

She could be preparing
for his routine business trip...
But see how the lips twitch,
the fingers clutch
as the body
almost straightens
then bends
like an old woman.

Now the boxes are taped
and tightly strung.
Carefully she marks
the contents on the brown tops.
She could be storing
the unused, the outgrown
in the attic...
Tidy with her years,
she throws nothing out.

A woman stares
at the sealed boxes.
A woman stares
at the emptied drawers,
the emptied closet
and begins, already, to move
what is her own
into these large holes.
A woman is practical
even in loss.

To Live as One

The days warm up, and then the birds.
At six o'clock they start their chords
that counterpoint inside my head.
They try to sing me out of bed.

All morning while the birds rehearse,
like a dimmer in reverse
the early light turns up to glare.
My room retains the winter air

and keeps an overcast all year.
As if to mock my lazing here
a jay unwinds from tree to tree
to show he's busier than me,

but for all his busyness
I can't discover what I miss.
The trees grow younger as I look.
A tiny starling in the oak

is already pecking his way to spring.
There must be some prodigious thing
I should be moving from or toward,
some needing done that I've ignored,

somebody's need that I could fill
and filling fill the time I kill
watching birds come and go.
The girls away at school outgrow

my mothering, and lately me.
Like the starling in the trees
they rush towards seasons of their own.
Their father has a separate home.

Two songs in modulated keys
intersect from distant trees.
And now the lusty syllables
close in in mating rituals.

I've known a few men in my life,
was even made by one a wife
and then, in loneliness, another
let me take him as a lover.

From them I learned one thing that's true:
a loneliness comprised of two
is lonelier than one alone.
I've told all the men I've known

I have discovered better ways
not to occupy my days.
Now they don't call me anymore.
Some things a season can restore,

as girls return to men their youth.
There is a lie in every truth.
I stay in bed and watch time pass
like nervous motes across the glass.

I tell myself I am content
to be a self-made indolent,
to live as one until I die.
A seed of truth in every lie.

Ghost Town

Everyone here has left or died:

the boy that cried, scraping
like a knife
against my nights;

the man who smiled but said "no,"
(he wanted out,
he was glad to go);

and the children,
those slippery, thankless things
who pitched their lives like coins far from here.

Slowly the buildings lie down
or strip to sticks. One match
would flame this town to a thimble of ash.

But the boy, he bagged all the matches,
sharp-edged metals, glass and ropes,
laughing, for the first time, his way out.

The children spoke of the cities they would make.

I keep thinking they will write, confessing,
"Any place is like any place, if you stay
long enough," or, "we're all right...will keep

in touch." But nothing touches this town.
Picked clean, its shanties breathe
airy as rib cages, a souring wind

whines down the dusty streets
I cannot recognize
or leave.

The Difference

A gull circles for the joy of circling
moving, now and then, a corrective wing
or tilting to catch a current's ride,
he shifts his easy shoulder into glide
(as if that's all you need to do to fly)
and climbs and climbs the sweetness of the sky
until diminished to a speck of flight
then grows in gracefulness back into sight.

Beneath his vast, solitary arcs
crows flit like nervous question marks
back and forth in peripatetic packs.
Someone should teach crows how to relax,
Fast and hard they stitch between trees,
fighting themselves by flying against the breeze
as if flight were just a way to get somewhere.
In letting go, the gull's already there.

The Great White Heron

The heron balances his bulk
on one insubstantial leg,
then compacts his wings and neck
to shape his body like an egg.

As if to say the world's too much
(whether too right or too wrong)
he meditates above the marsh
and closes out the raucous throng

that boomerangs from bank to bank.
Against the nervous greenery
his white ellipse is like a blank,
an absence in the scenery,

a form abandoned by the mind.
But just as he seems to turn to stone
and fix a thing so well defined,
he fills the hollows of his bones

and lifting loosens out the ring
in a slow release of neck and head.
And the whole world diminishing
under his white wing spread.

The River

Plain following fancy, two ducks
(now floating, now wading, now stuck)
trail a fine line of rivulet
down the middle of the muddy inlet.

Like a run in silk the line spreads.
Then the word, as from the river's bed
feet unstick to dangle or paddle free.
Ten more come floating in, their wake of V's

echoing the arc on arc of waves
that push in scalloped rows into the cove.
All day the river climbs while the embankment
(haphazard shelves of rubble and cracked cement)

seems to sink back into layers of silt.
As if some instinct set the basin atilt
just at the moment it had filled to brim
and one more drop might overflow its rim,

in one quick turn the waves shift to reverse,
turning the ducks around on the river's course.
Steadily it drains to shallow tub
of muddy brine. And then, plain mud.

Stronger than my need to keep things full,
the river has its own and deeper pull.
Twice each day it makes an outward track.
Unlike most human things, it twice comes back.

from
NAMING THE DARKNESS

Road Publishers, 1991

Country Relics

Nothing is scrapped.
Rusty as hens,
plump-bellied Fords,
the old Deeres
of tractor and plow
root where they stalled.
They mark the land
like headstones.
Even the earth
with its screen of weeds
cannot claim them.

Nothing is torn down,
carted off.
Weak-kneed, abandoned
barns tilt, open out
airy ribs. Scarecrows
staying against wind
and nevermore,
why don't they fall?
Like memory, wisteria
climbs their splintery limbs
in purple skirts.

And the old homesteads,
gutted, absent
as the soft eyes of cows,
still stand.
Silent patriarchs,
they look down
on the latest crop:
generic tins
of mobile homes; satellite
dishes set
on invisible fields.

Side-Show

I can still hear
the barker's chant
snagging curious
boys into his tent.

Outside, a gallery
of nightmares. Frame
by frame he baited us
and sang their names:

Human Snake (watch him
light his own cigar!),
Pin-Head, Dog-Child
(preserved in a jar),

She-Man, Faceless Wonder...
He took our change, waved
us into a dark world,
then paused, as in a cave,

to let our eyes adjust.
It smelled of dirt, apple bins
gone rotten in Grandpa's cellar,
sweat and grown up sin.

I had to strain to see
then quickly drop my gaze.
(Locking eye to eye,
I would be hexed.) Those days

we dared most anything
to be men. I remember
the walk home, cursing
stones across the water.

The Fat Man

Imagine the sea
drained to salt;
imagine its thirst,
the inpulling
ache that dreams
of wind and rain
washing earth,
trees, towns
into its mouth.

If he could
he would devour
the world whole,
eliminate nothing.

Eating, he brags,
is his living.
Before crowds
he packs in
a village feast,
then stomps
the bone-heaped
dirt for more.

Day and night
from his king's chair
he cries, "I want!
I want! I want!"
to their scared,
averted eyes.

Seduction of the Great Sea Turtle

Pulled in, he hides
in a bone vest.
I imagine flesh
salted by seas, cooled
by a million moons.

I am not fooled
by his armor,
his dull wit.

I know the trick
of his pockets,
his loose collar.
If I breathe the ocean
into his ear,
feet dance, the fat
tongue flicks.
I can make
the lizard's eye
glow red, unpout
the grey mouth slit
with a kiss.

When I flip
his world, mount
his gold belly
and ride,
he is all mine.

Sleeping Beauty

Is this what the mad feel,
trapped in their bodies,
their minds,
like blind paralytics?

How long has it been—
months, years, centuries—
stalled in this dusk
where nothing touches me?

I imagine the weight
of sheets, dust
settling on each hair
of my flesh, a breath
floating by my bed.

I want to smack into walls,
fly out of trees, stub toes,
burn tongue or bleed again
from the needle's prick.

I am tired of waiting.
Waiting for what? The lie
I was given at birth
against the bitch's curse:
the god-man,
his one good trick
that will break me
into living?

Sometimes I hear
the briers grow, their dry
tongues weaving, weaving.

The Snorer

Women are afraid to sleep with me.

It is my snoring
        reminds them
of thundering hooves
        the snorting
of a penned beast
        death's rattle.

It is a dybbuk   they cry
who sings
        through my nose, my mouth
to curse them.

        They have appealed
to rabbis, holy men, the old ones
with their prayers and amulets.

        For brief spells
when my sleep is silent   they say
"The unheard and unseen
are most to be feared."
        They sit up waiting.

I have fasted
        taped my mouth
packed my nose
        with wadding
propped my head
        on stacked pillows
and slept   for a week
on the hard floor.

I have made myself sick with their fear.

It has come to me lately   maybe
they only imagine
        that I am snoring.
I have never heard myself snoring.

Maybe it is their fathers
            their bearded grandfathers
tribes of snorers   drilling
back through the years.

Maybe it is themselves they hear
and are ashamed
            quick to accuse
"You snorer!" "You noisy devil!"

The Bed

How I slump
from your weight,
grow lumpy and soft
like you,
and I'm half your age.
Just look
at these stains!
My skin splotched
by the spill of bodies
(Oh, the secrets
I could tell),
the glass that falls
with the world
from your grip.
The dead
sleep you rise from,
rinse off,
sours my heart.
I am sick
of your sounds:
the moaner
with her gift of salt;
the cat who throbs
deep in the belly,
a wishbone of sighs;
the hag
who burbles, snorts,
wheezes, farts.
You hold nothing back!
You let go, falling
even as I hold you,
carry you across.
Sometimes you reward me
with stillness,
the gentle wake
of your dream.

I relax. You turn
lunatic, thrashing,
climbing sideways
the steep air
until I can't breathe.
I am tired
of your demons, ghosts,
lovers, the darkness
that brings us together.
I am tired of being
this life you've made
and must lie in.

A Perfect Darkness

On a day that will last through winter,
a morning they call night,
they enter a perfect darkness,
they leave the light.

While outside life lets go
they hang themselves up, like clothes
out of season, by the ten
hooks of their toes.

Their dark umbrellas fold,
tuck in and disappear.
One drop, slowing time,
loosens in the air,

falls, as they fall into
themselves, deeper than dreaming.
Their minds empty like pockets.
They breathe without breathing.

For six months they hang,
silvered in silence
like soft formations, holding
the shape of their absence.

They wait without waiting
for the world to turn right,
to return to themselves
and the flawed dark night..

Love's Alchemist

I take what you are
and dress it in a dream—
embroidered cloth draped
on the cross of a rack.

I use what you give—
word, gesture, touch—
as splinters for a frame
the mind fills out.

When you speak
I catch the words I want.
I am free
to interpret the silence,

to name your fever,
to excuse your absence.
In my hat of stars
I am a conjurer.

Love's alchemist,
I change what you are—
transmute the frog,
spin gold from straw.

With what you cannot give
I fashion walls, a roof—
a little house of cards
to hold against the wind.

How They Use Me

I listen when they talk
about me. My name
flies into their speech,
their dreams.

They say I am blind,
call the man led
by a dog's eyes
my name.

Darkness or glare
cannot blind me.
I send my eyes out
like a song
that sings back.
I send my song out
like hands that touch
the shape and the place
of things.

I have watched them
stumble in the dark
woods at night.
When I fly past
they call me
black moth,
black leaf.

And the man lost
in the dark maze
of his thoughts,

the man who living
with stones becomes stone,
has my name.

Because they don't
know me, they say
I am many things:

across screens,
wings that blacken
a full moon;
a cape and teeth.

Women hold their white
necks in sleep, afraid
of wanting me.
I tangle in the loose
hair of their dreams.

I am not their dreams.
I am not their words.
I am what I am.

They need a name
for the darkness.
They take mine.

What We Wear for Men

Sometimes a smile
hard
as a plate's edge
when men say
smile
and our frowns
flip like fish
to swallow
their guilt.

Sometimes red
for lines
we would carve
on backs
like wounds
dragged across snow
but our nails
retract
against flesh
and the little
animals of our mouths
leave soft prints.

Sometimes black
hose, heels, lace—
the doll
we dress up
for the rumpled
centerfold
of their sheets,
the fantasy
we put on
for them
to take off.

Sometimes masks
that crack
like the wizened

faces of Indians,
ancient tricks
of make-up, dyes,
scents, beads
to adorn
the plain sack
of our nakedness.

June Birds

Almost every day now it happens—
that splat against glass.

Seen from outside, these large
windows of my stucco house
float a mirage of trees and sky

like rooms mirrored to repeat themselves.
How they repeat themselves!
Since sunup, a party line of old news

ricochets, tree to tree. Now one
sounds his single song from the elm;
distant pines are a choir of mimicry.

Like lovers constantly needing
to reassure each other, themselves,
they give to get back.

Only the pitch, the emphasis alters,
as in "I *love* you": "I love *you.*"
Any phrase, repeated enough,

is a small death. Undressed
and jeweled in white, I find them
silent in bushes, in beds,

or sometimes, on the cement steps,
only dazed and leaking
burgundy under the belly.

Daft by the berries' wine, June days
they sail blind. Lured by the bird
that blooms on a pane of glass,

like the body's echo
soaring back into itself,
they break whole on impact.

Loving you is like that.

To Young Men, to Make Time

First, there's the one about fish...
They're a dime a dozen. Why waste
all your lines on one tail? Life's
too short. A man could starve
picking the same bones each night.

Variety's the spice... Give me a hot
redhead, a luscious blond, a racy
brunette to keep me cooking. A change
of pace is what men need to stir
up interest. Try anything once

but don't get in too deep. Ignorance
is bliss and familiarity breeds...
Given free reign, she'll talk
your head off. A quick roll in the hay
is all you need. Enough's enough.

Now for the catch. Promise her
everything (the moon and stars, etc.).
If she won't bite, don't give up
the ship. There's more where that one
came from. Remember about the fish.

For the Good Children

This is a special park
fenced only in trees
reserved for the very good
who are not heard or seen,

who play at hide and seek
(so innocent, they hide
behind shut eyes
and never peek),

and never wander off
to lose themselves in woods
or tease the river witch.
They are so good

who never cry or whine
or want. For toys—
blocks of stone, lambs
that make no noise,

and dolls with wings
to fan their dreams who nap
beneath their names
and "Gone to Sleep,"

as if it were a place
across a yard at dusk
from which a mother's call
could start them back.

Beneath the oak, cross-
legged, the women sit,
and softly talk,
and knit.

They wait with a stony
patience—not granted men,
from darkness to sunlight
to darkness again.

Daughters

Rain. No rain. Every year
on the anniversary they come.
Can you hear them
padding around (inspecting
the grass, maybe), talking?

Such nice things they say.
(It's like voices heard
under water.) Such blessings!
As if all the bad
(so whose life was perfect?)
sinks a little each year.

See how they leave
small stones beside the big stone?*
Such a pile I have
(you should excuse the expression)
would make a pharaoh proud!

Poor Rose next door
with her one son
and bubkes for stones.
How many years ago I told her,
"Ai, Rose, daughters! Daughters!"

*It is Jewish custom to place a small stone on the headstone when
visiting a grave.

Lament

In a crook of pine
she sits, puffed
with old apologies.
Something like,
"I'm sorry," pause,
"Why me?"

Close by, in pairs
cabbage butterflies
do tricks,
spiral up or zigzag
through the air
like limericks.

But the dove sits
talking to herself.
The sound—
a blue flute
or the lingering throb
of a wound—

leaves and returns
all day to the grey
cage of her chest.
She stays perched, as if
on a nest

of empty eggs.
She fills
with whines.
The weight of her song
keeps her
steady in the pine.

The Egret

He stands above
his inverted brother
like loosely seamed
halves of a heart.

The beak that breaks
water, flipping silver,
might be a kiss. To kiss
one's own mouth

in green mirrors,
stabbing at love
to swallow death!
How we die

to love ourselves
through each other,
a desperate applause
of clapping flesh

that leaves us
stinging, bereft—
like, now, the egret
who rises, who drowns.

With Difficulty the Poet Dissolves
His Love Affair with Prosody

There is another woman.

I say this first, knowing
it will break
your inclination to argue.

No, she is not comely,
not in the classical sense
like you. Nor can she effect
the glissando of gestures
you perfect. She'd rather
listen to the babel of traffic
than a dusty quintet or the movement
of water slipping over rocks
beneath the engorged stars
of mountain nights. So what!

Everyone else approves.
Our friends like her
for her, how should I put it,
eclectic keeping up,
her daring, her unaffected
nakedness. She swigs
Milwaukee from a can
and with unapologetic gusto
burps. How natural!

More changeable than petulant,
she tries on moods
like a woman in a dressing booth.
No silk kimonos, French perfumes,
candle-lit dinners, or courtships
of centuries spent kissing
for this doll.

Extended foreplay, like conjuring
up the muse, she likes to say,
is a waste. She's so direct.

You call it middle-age crisis,
the lure of short skirts
and perky breasts.
Call it what you like.

You'll get over it. There are still
plenty of young men taken
by the solid charms of older women.

I'll be back, you say?
Don't hold your breath!

from
LIGHT PERSISTS

University of Tampa Press, 2006

Early Farm Road

—Sweet Briar, Virginia

Laboring up a road
that went from black to clay,
I passed the quiet fields
where cows graze.

The road became a cut.
On either side, my eyes
kept going, leaping
into shadow.

And then the woods
stopped, the hills fell off
around me. I stood
in an openness,

stunned still
in a sky-swept place
where time and the world
dropped away

until I was nothing
but joy, the joy
of something small
loosening into space.

I would have stayed
and built a house
inside that stalled pitch
but I had known

other times like this—
at the ocean's edge,
on a mountain
wrapped in stars,

or, once, in the dark
cathedral of a foreign city
where I lived
and could not live.

The Cormorant

Have you known him—
the one who seams
the elements in his wake?

The sky falls
on his head,
there is fire
in his eyes,
the river opens
and closes
on his neck.

Have you known
the falling
which is not
falling
but the head
dreaming down
through darkness
to the place
of the body?

Have you known
the pull
of the bottom
and the silver
of the bottom
and the black mud
of the bottom
and the ache
of the one
who stays gone
so long
the waves
erase him?

And have you felt
the light

reach down
to claim you—
and did you rise
like a charmed snake
somewhere else?

The Wait

Where one world ends
and another begins
she sits, as all waiting sits,
on an edge.

Wrapped in her wings,
she has planted herself
on an apron of grass
at the bulkhead's rim—

a starting line of sorts.
To cross is to fall or fly,
claim water or air
over her squatter's portion.

Rain falls. Hours and weeks fall.
The tide comes in and goes out
like hunger.
She won't be moved.

Nearby, day and night
nearby, her loosely
anchored mate shuttles
between the banks of her vision.

Naturally, she pretends
not to see him, to be so
caught up in her own doing,
which to the eye is nothing,

but you *know,* you *feel* her
pouring her heat down
evenly as the sun on creation
as her neck and head

throw a black question
mark into the river
where, like all questions,
despite its weight it floats.

Memorial

—After a painting by Jan Saudek
from *Love, Life, Death Other Such Trifles*

She left her clothes
folded at the foot of her bed.
She had shaved her head
earlier that morning and left
her hair by an open window
for birds to soften
their nests. She left
her money and her keys
and her name in her purse
on a countertop.
Just like that—
she walked out
of her house
and out of town
and she would have kept walking,
pushed along by a gentle hand,
but the wind had other plans.

When she came to a wall
of earth-colored rock,
there was no going over or around,
and she was tired,
relieved to be stopped.
She stood before the rock face—
as many times she had stood
naked before mirrors
or the appraising eyes of men—
and gave herself over
to the cool reflection
of all she would become.

Doubt

One week of cherry blossoms,
one perfect summer's day
in April and I'm a fool for faith.

The goose sits on her nest.
Seed by seed, blackbirds
take religion at the feeder.

The dove mounts the dove;
mid-air, the fly rides the fly.
From a sky dusted in pollen,

pines lay their green shadows
down upon the river.
If I throw off my rags

would I stand, weightless
at the land's end, ready
to cross over?

Where Is the House?

Where is the house that will hold them?
Not his house with its one room.
Love would keep bumping into itself.
Love would shrivel and bruise.

And the things in her house,
like cats who have adjusted to one mistress,
would grow uneasy. How could love live
in a house of sighing cushions?

It must be a third house, a house
for this third person, them.
But where will she go when she aches
in all her corners to loosen loneliness?

But where will he go when he longs
for the dance of the bones in the howling place?
O the love that would fall in on itself!
O the love that would fly apart!

Where is the house that can hold them?

The Moronic Ox: A Fable

Because he hated the brand
of the sun on his back
and having dirt on his feet
even on Sundays
and found a life
braced to a groaning weight
was getting him nowhere

and because he dreamed of seas
of grass and the pool
of a shade tree
where he could lose himself
in the anywhere of song

when he refused to work the fields
the villagers called him
a good-for-nothing
who would set
a dangerous example

so they tried him
and found him guilty
of plotting to overthrow
what their bones knew—
that life is its own burden,
a blind pulling from birth to death—

and then they turned him
on a spit and feasted
and carried him
in their bellies to the fields.

The Parrot-Ox

The parrot-ox
is clearly confused
as evidently
so were his parents.

Being both heavy and light
he can neither
fly nor roost,
which makes his life

a kind of hovering
between two things
that cross each other out.
All play is work,

all drudgery is sport,
and so he spends his days
busily doing nothing,
circling square

fields of thought
like a practical idealist.
At night he holds forth
in a neighborhood bar

in his undertaker's suit
and Indian headdress.
He drinks to sober up
and tell again

the sad joke
of how we die at birth
into opposites.
And then he laughs

till he cries and cries
till he laughs,
sorrow and joy
mixing it up in his blood.

Dog Days

They knew it was Sirius,
those ancients who sat
stuporous in their sticky sheets,
too zapped to peel a grape

but not to kick the dog.
Someone had to take the rap,
and so they hurled their curses
at the heavens, only backwards:

Mad dog! they cried, aiming
for the mutt at Helios's feet,
not daring to incur the real heat
of the big dogs, the Olympians,

who also sat, lolling
on their soggy clouds,
too whipped to fight or cheat
or meddle in men's folly.

The Life That Goes on without You

Some days are like cows
following each other's tails
into pasture. It's raining.
You linger in bed
leafing through a book
the way you undress
a head of cabbage.
When the clock's
hands clap at noon,
your clothes
lay themselves out
like admonishing friends.
What's the use, your mind says
as your body moves.
The cats are fed,
the laundry
washed and folded.
Strangers drop in
through a mail slot.
Somebody pays the bills.
Or doesn't. Somebody
steers the car that returns
with its perishable cargo.
Hunger fixes dinner.
Full of itself, the garbage
walks out of the house
and doesn't come back.
It's still raining
in your head.
Black rain now.
Biblical.
In the living room
from a wealth of channels,
you can enter
any life you choose.

Cancer Ward Game

It's a game—something to kill time,
Death explains. The solarium is bathed in light
and Sister Margaret is watering the white flags.

When you get there, he says, then pauses
for suspense—*if you could be with anyone...?*
Their eyes roll up. They are rummaging for names.

Are we limited to those who are history?
the newcomer wants to know,
or can we take our favorites with us?

You some kind of pharaoh? says Abe.
From her turban, Mrs. Esposito pulls a hairless
Chihuahua. *Pepe,* she croons and strokes her lap.

Before long, the sunlit parlor is crowded,
Elvis, Jesus, the Marx Brothers
mixing with their own beautiful dead.

Everyone is excited, talking at once. More arrive.
They are kissing and hugging, the rear doors
of their gowns flapping, *Come in! Come in!*

My Daughter the Thief

It started with
makeup, hose,
earrings—
little things
she thought
I wouldn't miss.

Don't look at me!
she said—
like I was losing
my mind.

Then one day
when I wasn't looking,
she took
my breasts,
my hips.

Now she sneaks
out at night
who knows where
in my best dress.

Here I am
lying in bed
and my dress
is dancing,
and my hips
are shaking,
and who knows
what kind
of intoxicated,
filthy mind
keeps pawing
my breasts.

Another Time

I was delivering my daughter
to college. Everything
eighteen years can gather
was the dragging weight

of the U-Haul. For ten hours
she slept, curled
away from me, her buttocks
up against the shaft.

Was she gearing up for some
reckless future? What was
I thinking! Along the way
there are places

that beckon us to stop, or warn—
last chance! When I knew
my mother was dying,
when I saw her shriveling

around a hardness
that ached to be revealed,
we talked about everything
unimportant. It was easy—

two routes falling
west and south to empty out
in Atlanta. The next day
I moved her in. I did what

mothers do. It was work.
Hard work. Sometimes
the body is the only
way we have.

The Visit

There were two of them
as if what they carried
was too heavy for one.

They stood in the doorway,
dark blue uniforms
backed in light.

Their faces were not sad or happy.

They asked to come in.
They had something to tell her.

Was she alone?
Was there anyone they could call
to be with her?

They told her to sit down.

Together they pulled
from their mouths
the name of her daughter.

Together they placed
the unbearable weight
in her lap.

Sharing Grief

We pass it back and forth
through telephone wires.
We divide it
into boxes—
yours, mine.
We compare the forms it takes
in the foreign countries
inside us.
Each day it is different;
each day it is the same.
Together,
we plant rocks.
Together,
we throw out
the empty hooks
of interrogatives:
Why *her* and not another?
Why not *us*?
Why like *that*?
Not "Why," time teaches us
but "Is." If death is
nothing but the end
of the accident of living
we must learn to let go
of the universe
spinning a hole in our palms.

ed Bud

—Planted in memory of my daughter Jessica

his third spring, a blush,
arely a tinge of pink,
ooked from a thin branch.

have known them
wild in the mountains,
the first splashes of color
in the blue woods.

Again this summer
the few leaves, bitten
by blight, singed by sun,
hang like sick hearts.

Birthday on Brokenback Mountain

Late morning with only
the woods for neighbors,
I sit naked on the porch
and watch the sun unfurl

your gift of sixty roses.
Petal by slow petal, they relax
as all around cicadas
empty and refill—their chirr

so constant the hours forget
to notice. Late August and already
a litter of yellow leaves
brightens the forest floor.

Through glass doors:
the camber of your hip,
the gentle rise and fall of your
shoulder in disheveled sheets.

I remember your gift
of lacy nothings, lovemaking
that saw the stars go blind
in grey light. I remember

when I was little
I knew my grandmother was born
in a full-body corset
and heavy, black lace-up shoes.

Her upper arms flapped
like laundry on a line. Now
my daughter carries a child
who will rename me.

Cornflower, phlox, ox-eyed daisy
plucked from a field guide—
Later we'll walk these woods
with the comfort that comes

from addressing a thing
by its name. *Jane,* I say out loud,
Jane. It feels good—
this wind washing over me,

the sun climbing my back,
easing the arguments of bone,
the proximity of you who turn
toward me even as you sleep.

Counting Blessings

I no longer feel the compulsion to iron.

I can have any color hair I want.

I can indulge in the comfort
of white cotton underwear.

I have a better chance to be taken
seriously by men.

Like a dress that made me happy
when it hung two sizes too big,
my skin has become commodious.

I have grown to appreciate
the steadfastness of sleep.
When did another come nightly
and hold on for eight hours?

Everything is still possible
in dreams.

I get to revisit those I only thought I knew
decades ago in books.

Reading glasses are cheap.

The body keeps on
reminding me we are together in this.
Each new ache is a recommitment of vows,
an implicit faithfulness.

I am grateful
for the wisdom of the bowels,
how they know what to keep
and what to throw away,

I still have most of my teeth.

Thanks to the dilating holes
in memory's pockets,
there is less to keep track of.

My Honda has memorized the way.

I am no longer driven
by hormones to ride
roller coasters and bumper cars.

No one is pushing me on stage.

I have traded the cliff's edge,
conflagrations of the heart, rapids,
for what is still at the center:

the mind content in its hammock
to watch thoughts drift
and change shape like clouds.

There is no one left
to tell me how to behave.

Some places give discounts.

from
THE RED COAT

FutureCycle Press, 2013

How to Start a Day

Begin by letting go of the hem
of your dream. Let it slip
backwards into a black lake
as you greet the dawn. Be thankful
for small aches. You have survived

night's heavy arms to wash yesterday
from your face. Begin to create
the opus of a new day. Look out
from a kitchen window as you savor
a first cup of coffee. House wrens

flap at the feeder. A squirrel
dances osiers so that the willow
shakes with laughter. Be thankful
for the small favors of sunlight
walking across the lawn, a cabbage

butterfly teasing the azaleas,
the pink rain of cherry blossoms.
Even the neighbor's dog barking
ducks from his yard is sacred.
Open to morning's hymns:

the big mouth of the garbage truck,
the mockingbird's purloined songs,
chatter on the corner waiting
for the yellow school bus. The engine
of the day purrs in your throat

as you dress. Sweep your calendar
clean of doctor appointments,
chores. The vacuum and the duster
can wait. Let the day surprise you.
Be thankful to be who you are.

Constitutional

As a child, it was my job
to follow our terrier's nose
around the block. Now,

for forty minutes each day,
I walk the old dog
of my bones, a happy vessel

for wind and sun,
lemony scent of magnolias,
confluence of bird song.

A cardinal swoops down
to preen in the rainbow-
spattered spray of a sprinkler.

Two boys in caps, like birds
with their bills on backwards,
blur by on skateboards.

An automobile honks
geese to the side of the road.
I hum as I walk. I am never alone.

My shadow knows when to lead,
when to keep beside me,
when to follow me home.

The Imagined Man

I thought of him on my way home
from visiting my daughter in Florida.

I gave him features, a pastiche of parts
that had attracted me to others.

I dressed him from Saks. To please
my children, I made him Jewish.
I named him *Henry.*

I gave us a history. Recently met,
we frustrated our waiter by kibitzing
for hours before ordering.

We saw each other when we talked.
We let the past be past.

Later, instead of fingering popcorn,
we held hands in the movies.

Teenagers again, we necked
on a bench at the waterfront
under the tipped smile of the moon.

Our bodies vibrated after touch
like tuning forks.

I was about to slip into lingerie
when the plane landed in Norfolk.

Contemplating *Lovers in the Red Sky*

"It's always the first time," you like to say
afterwards. From our still-warm bed I stare
at Chagall's lovers afloat on a day
that lasts forever. Impossibly, they share
one body, a sacred knot. He never
leaves for work. She never returns below
to the house in town to cook their dinner.
They never argue. They will never grow
apart from the tedious wash of years.
Bathed in the red glow of an always sun-
set, they suspend transfixed above the fears
that plague the rest of us. Clocks reclaim the hours.
I worry about dinner. You rise to shower.

Hiking Brokenback Mountain

The trail was narrow. I followed you up Brokenback
Mountain like a stunted shadow. I carried
my field guide for wild flowers, their names—tokens
of their faces: black-eyed Susan, butterfly weed,
foxglove. The path was steep. I had to walk
slowly, catching breath, and fell behind. It took
a while for you to notice. On hikes you never talk.
You lose yourself in the grandeur of where you look;
that day—the sun filtering through the fire
of turned leaves, the outcroppings of limestone
stippling the mountainside, a hawk's sweep. The air
was crisp with frost. I had never felt more alone
than on that mountain. I should have known better.
Nothing would be in bloom in late October.

The Red Kayak

You nosed the red kayak into
the river; we glided blind
through a thick screen of fog.

I was behind you. Your arms
worked while I sat still in the
haze of last night's argument.

You had packed everything
you thought we'd need to return
to the garden: stargazer lilies,

my favorites; scented candles,
our music, wine. I'd packed
lingerie in a suitcase of doubt.

The sun rose, burning off the fog.
I know what I want! you had said.
I stared at the life preserver

on your back. My arms grew
tired, drawing wheels in and out
of the water. The only sound,

a honking trail overhead.
We had used up our voices
exhuming the past.

In the kayak, we were
aimed 90 degrees toward
that thin, black horizon.

Tour Guide in the Musée du Louvre

—After *La Grande Odalisque* by Ingres

It's the torso we see first, its languid,
sweeping curve that lures us in. Let critics
argue the deformation of the arm,
the extra vertebrae, the too small head;
the body's seduction is no less perfect.
The rondure of the breast, the buttocks
are like ripe fruit beckoning to be taken.
Dressed in a jeweled turban and bracelets,
she holds a peacock fan, its many eyes
against her thigh. As if to repeat a theme,
we're next drawn to her gaze—aloof—
as if the years of harem life have worn her down.
Imagine holding this pose for hours...
Maybe it's the end of a day and she's masking
a stiff neck, the chill of a drafty studio, hunger,
restlessness. Or perhaps she's just taken
a toke of opium from the hookah by her feet,
withdrawn to a foreign place we cannot reach.

Le Déjeuner sur l'herbe

I'm not embarrassed. No, my fixed stare
suggests only that you're interlopers on the scene.
Oh years ago I could rouse a media storm.
Today my nakedness seems nominal. Clean

country air; a tipped basket of fruit,
a knot of bread; for cloth, the sweet
summer grass—this outing is a holiday from
my cramped flat, heat-swollen city streets.

A friend came with me. By the sun-lit bank
you'll find her, just risen from a bath,
slipping into a white chemise. Surely you've
entered into places like this, where faith

distills your life to one shimmering afternoon
and lets you rest there. But Manet tried
to warn us about opposites. Since you've
stayed, baffled by the canvas, I'll confide

there is something indelicate here. Business
suits at a picnic! Our dates refused to remove
their jackets and cravats. One stares off, bored,
into the distance. My suitor in the hat reproves

critics of the latest exhibit at the Salon
des Refusés as if I weren't here. Their
presence makes me more naked than I am.
Visitors to the museum can't help but stare.

After *The Loss of Virginity*

In Gauguin's painting, the maiden lies naked,
stretched out on the earth like a corpse.

> Afterward, I covered myself with a white sheet
> as he rose to shower and dress.

She holds a wilted iris in her right hand.
Everything in the canvas is something else.

> We were going to be married that summer.
> Mother had selected daisies for the altar.

Her left hand embraces the evil-eyed fox
who places his paw on her heart.

> My parents were pleased. Following my romance
> with artists—a sensible lawyer.

Her eyes are closed and her feet cross
like Christ's on the crucifix.

> He slipped into business talk. He had maps
> in his shoes, money in his mouth.

The villagers move off to church or to a wedding.
The red fields of Le Pouldu are harvested.

> I dressed while he planned our future:
> where we'd live, what cars we'd drive, our two children.

One cloud in the blue sky, an echo of the maiden's body,
suspends in the heavens like a cry.

The Death of the Poet Li Po

Some say it was the wine. Some say it was love,
the moon smiling up at him from the river.
He was drunk. The boat was tipsy. He stood,
aching to embrace such loveliness forever.

The stars looked on. The lapping waves
were dancing. Leaning out over the gunwale,
he toasted his image which lay now beside
the moon's face and drank again. The sails

billowed and the little craft rocked him forward.
He could not deny himself. He reached and reached
until the river opened its mouth and drank him.
The boat was lost in the blackness. The beach

was far away. This was Li Po's last line.
Some say it was love. Some say it was the wine.

Sergei Aleksandrovitch Esenin's Last Poem

Here's the night table with its lit candle.
Here the looped rope dangling from a pipe
like a question mark or a hand-held
strap on a crowded bus. I am going on a trip.

Not far away. One step. One small kick,
a little dance and the light goes out.
I am sick of the industry of living, sick
of sleepless nights. Elizaveta, no doubt

true to your word, unopened my poem
written in the wine of my blood
sits in your pocket like a worry stone.
No stitched brow. No flood

of tears. A last breath, the psyche flies.
Goodbye, my friend, goodbye.*

*The first line of Esenin's poem

Blind Girl Talking to a Tree

Rough-skinned, wider
than my arm's embrace,
give me your name
so we can be friends.

I'm told you reach
higher than my house,
your limbs busy with leaves.

Tell me their shape and color
though I will never know color.

You don't have to tell me
about birds that make a home
in your branches.

I know them by their songs.

Tree, tell me what it feels like
to lose something
one leaf at a time.

Tell me what it's like
when snow comes
and the flood of darkness comes
and I'll say, *I know, I know.*

Stillness and Patience

Again this morning
at the yard's edge,
out of a blue nowhere
the heron appears,

flicking feathers,
spraying sunlight,
tucking wings and head
into a soft egg.

When the river is ready,
a foot or so high,
and the mud beneath
busy with movement,

she flounces down
as if to root. Stillness,
she knows, is the secret.
Stillness and patience.

She listens to her eye,
lifting one leg-stick,
then another,
so slowly her body

seems to float in place.
A dark sister, her reflection
in the tannin-stained river
rides beside her as

now! and now! she strikes,
skewering desire.

A River Would Never Insist

that the life of its banks
bow to its great body
or that the earth yield
to its hunger.

It would never presume
to swallow rocks, trees,
towns, humble stars
or proselytize to fish.

Time has shown it the way
all things follow on their own.
It has no motor;
it goes by letting go

and never stops to question
what greater power pulls it
or what moods its marriage
to the elements will expose.

It gushes, streams, walks
in its sleep, gallops, leaps,
trusting in the alchemy
of moon, tide, weather.

Blackbirds

Like loosely stitched
    scraps of cloth
        the wind shakes,
they sweep the sky,
      swarming and swirling
        this way,
    that way,

then drop down
      to blacken a field,
        to crown a tree,
        or facing
into the wind
      on telephone wires,
  to line up
    like musical notes
        in the same key,
as if to instruct us
    on the interconnectedness
        of all things.

The Egret

You arrive on the river alone, not alone
like a widow or an abandoned house—

more like a hermit content on his mountain
to be partner to the woods.

How slowly, methodically you move
so that beneath the still surface

what blue crabs or silver fish see
is a black reed lifted and lowered like a quill.

Safety, they read as your keen eye
signals the stiletto of your bill.

You are so good at nourishing yourself.
Afterwards, on one leg at the land's end,

you slip into the perfect white ellipse
of a meditation.

Japanese Cherry Blossom

Such abundance of a nothing weight!—
each blossom fully opened yet holding on.
Now a squirrel dances, thin limb to limb,
and the whole tree shivers. And now
a cardinal alights in his swashbuckler's habit
to breakfast on a delicacy. Tomorrow
the wind will begin its scattering work
and it will rain pink petals for a week.
As reverie follows bliss, green will follow pink.
And green can live for months on memory.

After Fire

Above a ruin of trees, crows stream.
There is music in their wings,
a peculiar lilt to their fragmentation
of grief. The moon balances
on a blackened branch where, of late,
an owl sat. Deer have scattered.
Where did the squirrels and voles hide?
Their prints mark the ashen ground
like hieroglyphs. Now the wind comes
to soothe. From nowhere, a cardinal
blazes—a red gash on a black canvas,
so beautiful the stars cry.

Winter Storm

She woke to white fields and a screen of snow
so thick she could barely see the shed.
He had left early. There was another place
he had to go once night fell. Tree to tree, a red

cardinal stitched the white air.
The garden that had worked her hands
all spring and summer lay buried. She felt sad
this morning, looking out on so much land

that held nothing. She would always wake
with a cold place beside her in the bed.
He would always return to the house in town
for the children's sake. She had read

the winter storm was coming. She was prepared
to wait it out. The distance between, a backroads
route, would go unplowed for days. She stared
at the dwarf maple, bent low by its heavy load.

The white-roofed feeder swung in the wind
like a ghost's lantern. She told herself it was good
enough that he wanted her. Before he left,
he had chopped and brought in wood.

Never Will Come Again

Never will come again
wishing on the head of a dandelion
when home was a safe place
in the spring that promises everything.

Never will come again
keeping vows lovers make
when the red-throated hummingbird
hovers over bluebells in the summer.

Never will come again
the mind that knows its way
when forests flame
and birdcall pulls south in the fall.

Never will come again
my daughter, lying still where snow
piles up to hide her name
in the bitter months of winter.

The Return

When the egret returned to the cove in March
she took it as a sign. How it kept walking
out of itself and emerging whole from its hunger.
It was a clear morning, the cherry tree shaking
into bloom over the tannin-stained river.
All winter she had been stuck as if at the bottom
of an abyss waiting for spring rain to pool
and float her up. Now this: the sun pouring in
and the waking wind; the egret pulling
the legs of the tide into her backyard
where the cherry tree bends to admire itself.
These were ladder rungs. So she climbed.
And the egret tucked the S of its neck
to its breast, unfolded its white wings
like an offering of good news, and lifted
into a gold-spattered, infinite blue.

The Long Life

There is no other that you are waiting for.
Everything you need is within your reach.
When the towhee sings his name in the maple tree
outside your window, sing back your name.
The wind will carry it downriver

to distant estuaries. Think of how hard
you have had to work to get to this moment,
how many soles you have discarded
along the way, how many moons have waned

like shuttered lanterns. Now you are light inside.
Now you have cast off parents, children,
a house, expectations, demands, politics.
You have earned the right to be self-ish.

Be like the heron who stands on the glistening
shoreline tucked into her wings.
Roam the countries in the two continents
inside your head. Speak to the natives,
all those people you have been and are.

All you have to do is listen.

Vows for the New Year

I will ride the day to new places,
reclaiming my child's wonder:
a buttercup's reflected face,

the falling star of a lightning bug,
the baton of a happy dog's tail.
I will smile easily and often, hug

the shoulders of each passing second
knowing it will not come again.
I will cultivate deserts, bend

sunlight to glister off sad highways.
I will make food my friend, not my lover.
I will walk three miles every day

and greet my neighbors. At sixty-eight
I will honor the body's complaints,
forgive mirrors their honesty.

I will wear gratitude like a red coat,
forbearing the shifting
seasons of hope and doubt.

from
IN THE SHADOW OF PARADISE

FutureCycle Press, 2017

Rousseau's Last Painting

This could be Eden, a realm of exotic,
lush vegetation, but the tree of knowledge
is missing, the snake that tempted Eve
slithers from the canvas, and a black man,
his loins brightly masked, replaces Adam.

This could be Paradise, its fruit forever
unspoiled on the orange tree, wild beasts
peacefully commingling, hypertrophic
lotuses perfuming the air, the enchantment
of birdsong and a flute's silvery sighs.

This could be a dream, the imagination's
longing for the impossible: a classical nude
on a red divan transported to a primeval
jungle. A lion's wide-eyed gaze invites you in.
You are the viewer. You are the dreamer.

The Siren and the Poet

—After Marc Chagall

Resting his head against the flames of the
Siren's tresses, the poet is beside himself.
Who better to instruct him on the art of voice,
so enchanting sailors could not resist?

A mermaid's tail replaces the wings of myth.
Pearls grace her neck. The poet's embrace
lifts her from the ocean as if he must pull
from his own depths the music of longing.

So like this Muse of the Lower World,
the poet sets sail across time's turbulent seas
to discover, *in spiritus,* the right music and
words to connect beauty, love, and death.

Soloist

Like an ornament
at the apex of a clay roof
a single bird will perch,
lord of the highest view.

This morning it's a dove
dissolving against the soft
grey of an overcast sky.
Better than high branches

or high wires, here he is
a soloist, rooster of the skies,
loosening his five-note aria
on the empty street below.

From my open window
in an adjacent building,
I sit watching, listening
to his abandoned heart,

thinking, this is the way
a poem writes itself,
note by solitary note
on the prevailing air.

Daphne's Plea

Help me, Father! Open the earth
to enclose me, or change my form.

I refuse to trade my woodlands
for the tomb of a marriage house.

Don't speak to me of grandchildren!

Bobolinks sing lullabies sweeter than I
who would rather romp barefoot
with the rabbit and the red fox

than be cracked open like a mollusk
to let Apollo in. These hips
were not meant to dandle babies.

Keep me safe, Father,
from the hard wants of a man.

If I must be rooted, plant my feet
in rich soil, let my womanly flesh
harden to bark, and let my limbs,

robust in sleeves of evergreen,
keep reaching for the sun.

Huis Clos

—After *The Joy of Life* by Paul Delvaux

In the clutch of what could have been
a slow dance, the couple are like boats
moored in the same berth
on a windless day.

Her hand will never leave the blue
mesa of his shoulder, his right arm
will never slip below her waist.

He will never feel her breath
on his neck, inhale her perfume,
or taste the red fruit of her lips.

Their legs will never rub against each other,
igniting a fire, because
it is impossible to dance in a painting.

Though the canvas holds a ballroom,
the world ends at its corners.

This is the torment Sartre warned us about:
Stalled in one place forever, a breath away
from everything you have ever wished for.

Cracks

If you look closely,
Mona Lisa's lips
are chapped
with cracks.

In Rilke's elegy
death zigzags
on a china cup.

Don't give me
perfection
immune to clocks.

Don't give me
the unbroken,
the safely stored
in airless vaults.

Every scar
is the shorthand
of an important story.

Each crack
is a door opening
onto a larger room.

Two Crows

Two crows lay on a bed of needles,
heads wrenched sideways,
wings splayed like broken fans.

I could read it as an omen,
one crow hurled from a great height,
but knowing, as gods do,
human resistance to dark signs,
a second plummeted to the ground.

I could call it a battlefield,
violence born of hubris or revenge
that ends with the heart bursting
its million feathers.

I could stage it as a tragedy,
the beloved shot from the sky,
the other, gutted by grief,
who sacrificed his life.

I could bury the crows in my yard,
but then my cat, or something cat-like,
would surely paw the dirt
to place an offering at my feet.

Adrift

How many times have you been adrift—
a small craft caught between the cataract
eye of the moon in a cloud-suffused sky
and the white-lipped ocean far from sure
ground? No paddles. No motor. No wind-
billowed sails to ride the swells home.

This happens, you know, even on land
when you stand, awash in sunlight,
a body in the company of other bodies,
relinquishing your soul to the
slap-slap-slap of waves on a hull.

A Sign from Above

—In memory of my daughter Jessica

Rudderless, windswept,
a Goodyear blimp
sails the skies.

Is anyone home steering
the great airship?

Clockmaker theorists
would argue
an abandoned design.

As a child
on my knees at night
I was taught to pray.
I believed *Elohim*
had ears and a heart
like my father.

In slow, relentless circles
the blimp repeats
and repeats itself.

Centuries ago,
mankind imagined
the angel-filled heavens
as an ocean with ports
offering safe passage.

I think of my daughter
driving home from college
while God slept.

Blue Nude

—After Pablo Picasso

We do not need to see her face. She has given us her back;
her turned-down head, cradled in her arms, rests upon knees
pressed to her chest as if yearning to return to the womb.

Is she crouched on a bare, cold floor in a vacant room, exiled
to a dream-like nowhere, or awash in the blues of Picasso's
own despondency. We want to know what disengaged her
from the world, hurt her into being an outcast. Did someone die?

Someone like a son or daughter the heart could not live without?
Was she betrayed by a lover? Or shamed by a sin committed
and found out? Perhaps her situation was desperate, bankrupt
of needs and decencies, starved by the indifference of fortune.

Because we will never know, we must look to our own lives.

On Happiness

A white boat plowing,
the prow lifting and lifting
where two black Labs
lean out, drinking
the rush of wind spray,
the man behind them,
his hair alive as wings,
his lips thrown back,
steering yet relinquishing
himself to something greater
than this bend of river,
his little boat, his two dogs.

Recalling the Blue Ridge in Summer

Sunlit, a thousand tinctures of green.
Up, up through fretwork, a sparrow's
clunky phrases, a cardinal's flames.
Rustling a tulip poplar's leaves,
the question marks of a squirrel's tail.
Through shrubby interstices, the white
flags of skittish deer. Along dirt trails,
hieroglyphic prints and steamy scat
of red fox, black bear. Rinsing the air,
the tiny mouths of violets. As if a name
could tame what's wild, black-eyed
Susan, bouncing Bet, butter-and-eggs,
Queen Anne's lace. Deep in shadow
where roots snake, like items dropped
in a fairytale, lady's slippers, Indian pipes.

In Defense of Stones

Blameless
against gravity,
blameless
in the hands of fury,
stones would just as soon
stay home
for a long nap.

They are not emotional
like seeds, leaves, the wind.
Yet, palmed
on a sun-glazed walk,
just one
can drive out loneliness.

Comfortable in a crowd,
or a castaway on beaches, roadsides,
what is more adaptable?

Willingly,
they let the river's tongues
soothe their edges

Willingly,
they join a community
to keep in, to keep out.

Balanced
one atop the other,
they show us the way
to stay calm, steady, secure
in the simplicity of being.

An Introvert's Love Letter to the Rain

All day you have tap-danced
on the roof, written on windows
with wet kisses as now and
again the sky spasmed. I love

how your mood spills into mine,
cautions me to keep tucked inside
myself while streets drown. I love
how you bless me, a mute doorbell,

time without hands, by the sofa
a book I've been meaning to read,
a carafe of chilled chardonnay,
and you (who else, my love,

knows me so well?) content
to be locked outside.

Rumination on Romantic Love

Romance refuses to sleep
its life away in the same bed.

When the storm hushes
and the landscape droops
to a tedious calm,
the heart plots its escape.

So we learn from Shakespeare,
Kierkegaard, Flaubert.

At the death of her affairs,
Madame Bovary chose arsenic—
antidote to a mediocre life.

Ophelia went mad. Juliet died
twice. I slough the past, waking
with windows thrown wide,

some days in the arms of love,
some days alone.

How We Happened

You arrived like a letter forwarded to a wrong address,
like a dog's nose to the ground seeking its way home,
like the last peach on a tree, or a stone skipped across
water to land safely in the palm of a leaf. You came

out of a seeming nowhere like a slow-developing sheet
of film; like a fledgling fanning the air from the lip
of its nest; like the sun, at day's end, content to bleed
into a purpled horizon. Like a bet decided on the flip

of a coin, *Heads,* you called. And I answered, the way
mourning doves volley songs through a stand of pines,
a bounced ball returns to a child's hand, or a stray
shadows a boy's heart to a door. Like a trumpet vine

to a hummingbird, I invited you in. *Stay!* I said,
Stay like a rock washed smooth by a river. And you did.

Arguments Against a Hearing Aid

I have no difficulty carrying on conversations
with myself. In dreams my hearing's perfect.

There's more room for silence—that stilled pond
upon which my best thoughts float.

Never one for idle talk, I get by with a head shake
and a smile. Eventually eyes, those quick learners,

pick up a second language. As for the world,
despair is a bottom feeder; it cups its ear

to bad news. Every day I reduce the number
of war dead, starving children, natural disasters.

I keep telling myself, you'll never miss
the dance of squirrels mornings on the tin roof;

behind the house, the kiss of the kingfisher
puncturing a hole in the Lafayette River;

the plucked heart of a Brahms concerto;
the vespers of birdsong in the pines.

Winter's Lessons

Trees stripped of summer's store
and fall's giveaway reveal the bones
of what stays. The river frozen

to the shore's lip speaks less,
keeps to itself what belongs to itself.
The bear in his den, the bat suspended

in his cave, know when to sleep
and when to wake. No longer
hitched to the world's rhythms,

no longer ruled by appetite, they wait
for an inner pull to rouse them.
And what is more instructional

than snowfall, its knack for making
the familiar new. Or night, arriving early,
flooding its borders at both ends.

How to Stage Regret

Hire your heart to edit your history
and overwrite the ego's scripts.
Remove all mirrors from the set,
those culprits of self-interest.

Let Mother Teresa direct
(who better to coach your actions!)
so that the casts' unspoken
needs guide your performance.

To circumvent stardom's pitfalls,
think of yourself as embodying
a cameo role. Let third-person
pronouns play the protagonists

as you wait in the wings for the chance
to support, praise, comfort, assist.
Avoid the temptation of finding
your person perfect, an exemplar

of compassion that would turn
selflessness into arrogance. Introduce
a Greek chorus in each act to express,
in wailing interludes, the apologies

you should have made. For audience,
the living and the dead: mother, father,
daughter, lover, friend—so that
at curtain's fall you may be forgiven.

A Brief History

When I was a girl
I wished for breasts.
I wanted lips
old enough
for Cotton-Candy-
Pink lipstick, for legs
a second skin
of silk, feet tipped
in the sinful slide
of 3-inch heels. Nights
I dreamed
a prince's kiss
would boot me
into living.

A young woman,
I flashed my hips
like whirligigs,
used bait:
a honeyed smile,
fishnet, leather,
black lace.
Lickety-split,
I caught a husband,
a house, two children,
pots and pans,
shopping lists,
calendars washed
in a sea of ink.

After the divorce, after
the children left, after
a string of lovers, after
Prozac, after
an analyst, after
I no longer
needed the mirrors

of men's eyes
or my name
in headlines, after
I gave away
designer labels
for gravity's housedress,

I found myself—
a woman
alone
on a mountain top
dancing naked
beneath the tipped
smile of a moon
and the winking stars.

Bedtime Imperative

Turn off the TV.
Turn off the lights.

Open the windows.
Open your hinged heart.

Let night enter,
black-faced, spilling
moonlight across the floor.

Turn down the covers.

Turn down the voice
of the caviller in your head.

Let go of lists.
Let go of your age.

Rejoice in the gift
of cool sheets.

Rejoice in the respite
of an unmanned skiff
adrift on a lake
strewn with stars.

Close your eyes.

Let curtains fall.
Let curtains rise.

Bella Donna

—After *Resting Somnambulist IV* by Pyke Koch

Let the candle go out.
Put the sewing machine to bed.
Do not worry. When you wake

sunlight will stitch the world back
to a motley quilt. Relax

as your mattress greens
with nightshade's leaves.

Feel yourself fall
into a delirium
beneath a chuppah of stars.

Bella Donna, here in this dream,
on this plain of death,
know you are truly alive.

Last Wishes

As I contrived a life
out of the box,
scatter my death
on the wind's back.

Let me live again
to mine the earth
in the belly of a worm.

For dirge, rain
on a tin roof,
a dog's yelp,
the laughter of leaves.

No make-up,
no touched-up
script for eulogy.

Say I was happily flawed.
Say I was human.

UNCOLLECTED POEMS

The Beauty of Abandonment

—Inspired by Daniel Pravda's
photography series, The Beauty of Decay

Off a dirt road in West Virginia,
set far back in a weed-infested field,
an abandoned wood-slatted home stands,
kneels really, in the shadow of the
Blue Ridge Mountains. I imagine

it is free of worries that wore
the floors thin, free of the coming
and going that loosened nerves
and hinges, free of cries and laughter
now that only the voice of the wind
comes to roam its empty rooms.

A rooster might alight on the rusty
tin roof, but his cock-a-doodle-doo
alarms only the interloping field mice
asleep beneath a cast-iron stove
or the wintering bats suspended
from rafters by the hooks of their toes.

In spring, wisteria will climb
the grey, sagging boards, peek in
through broken-out windows,
like a cover-up to apologize
for the family that moved their lives
into a shiny trailer closer to town.

I like to think the abandoned house
is happy, burden-free, collapsing into itself
like a body that has had enough of living
and is ready to let go, to relinquish
its heart to any weather, thankful
to be incrementally at home in nature.

Reflections on Irma

My head tossing, twisting,
shook by the big mouth
of the wind stripping me
leaf by leaf as I dug in

the gnarly toes of my roots
to keep fast in the earth,
my home for seventy years.
Beside me, like a death knell

I felt the sodden ground
tremble; a giant elm cracked,
snapped loose, crashed down
on a neighbor's roof,

terracotta shingles flying off
like startled birds. For two days
pitch as night, I kept telling
myself, "You have been

through this before, pounding
sheets of rain, wrenching gusts,
tornadoes, surging waves,"
as if wind and water conspired

to devour the entire world.
I've been through enough
to know every seed carries
its own death. I've been through

enough to know resurrection
even when my limbs were strewn
across a suburban battlefield
in the certain aftermath of sun.

Black Skimmers Abecedarian

Along the crashing and retreating shoreline
bathers on this blustering day would not
cross, a school of black skimmers, their heads
down flat or tucked along their backs, lay like an
ebony pool upon the white sand. Stilled, their
feathers riffled by heavy gusts, they slept,
grateful for the sun that had drawn them south.
Habit was in their blood. Each winter, before
icy winds undressed the trees, they didn't have to
join together to plot a path. Instinct, they
knew, was a better map, and lifted in unison
like a rain cloud streaming down the coast from
Maine to Florida, a caravan of "snow birds," to
nest in a warmth that kept bougainvillea roseate
on trees yearlong. Separate but close by, a
patch of gull-billed terns kept them company.
Quieted by the booming voices of wind and wave,
rarely did they stir or bark. I took a photograph, a
study in black and white, save for the yellow bill of
terns and the skimmers' slash of orange above an
uneven black beak. *Serenity in a Storm,* I'd call it, a
variation on the other "snowbirds," tourists
with their scampering, screeching children.
Xenial, the skimmers seemed unbothered by the
yelling above the wind or the kicked-up sand
zigzagging across the briefly borrowed beach.

What Spring Awakens

All night
from a high branch
the mockingbird
pipes
a medley of tongues.

He has marked
his territory
in a grove of slash pines
and now must wait.

Will she come?
Day after day
he wonders,
*Will I find my mate
in this sweet-scented place?*

Chack-chack-chack!
loosens from his throat
as he spies the one
he must chase
from earth to sky.

Then, in a dizzy dance,
they square off,
acrobats rising
and falling in air,

fanned wings
flapping to reveal,
like surrender flags,
white patches.

In an instant bond
their wings stall,
close like fans
as sixteen toes hook

on the same branch.
Quietly they perch,
whispering *hew-hew*
as night falls.

How to Make Friends with Wild Ducks

If you come often enough
to that place
where the earth hugs
a pond's perimeter
and keep your distance,
eventually you will become
part of the landscape.

If you come often enough
and sit statue-still,
content to be
an observing eye,
the space between you
will shrink.

If you come often enough
and bring treats,
they will come,
a waddling raft,
to greet you.

If you come often enough,
on a day
when you do not come
they will keep
listening for your footsteps.

Sometimes this even works with humans.

Spring Cleaning

The devils go first.
From corners, inside closets,
under my bed, inside my dreams
their ashes, like ghosts
of themselves, I sweep clean.

Next I attack drawers, shelves,
fouled linens, malodorous bins;
from the refrigerator throw out
hirsute pears, moldy cheese,
misstep's sour grapes;
send to the washroom the dirty
laundry of my brain.

Some demons beg to stay,
petition for permanence
in the storerooms of my heart
on the grounds of years of loyalty.

Rejected, they grow beards,
forked tails, talons, horns.
A pernicious bunch, to heckle me
they toss stink bombs in the toilet
of my hopes and fears.

Furiously, I dust, mop,
bleach, polish, trash meal
after meal for the hungry mouths
of garbage trucks.

When I'm finally purged,
lemon-scented and emptied out,
I am overcome by sadness.

Like footprints sucked from a rug,
a profound loneliness
haunts the immaculate
rooms of my house.

Because You Asked for a Happy Poem

I have scrubbed the rug using biodegradable
enzymes, swept up

the sharp stars that scattered a man's features
from the hallway mirror,

buried the blade, once used to chop vegetables
for soup, beneath the porch,

bleached the kitchen tiles where a weight
was dragged out, erased prints

from knobs, crazy-glued the heirloom china
tea caddy and cups, returned laps

to the uprighted dining room chairs, sucked
tears from the heavy curtains

that kept the windows blind, took down
wedding photographs that for years

marched up the stairs, watched the fire eat
a torn, bespattered shirt,

and flushed a gold ring down the toilet
before you even entered this poem.

A Savory Recipe

—For my daughter on her 16th wedding anniversary

I would never have thought sixteen years
a sweet anniversary, a rejuvenation of love.
That was the year your father and I divorced.

> I was confused as a child watching Mother pour
> sugar on seasoned meat. Like her marriage,
> I knew some things didn't belong together.

I have watched you and your husband
navigate differences, repair cracks and leaks
with the plug of sweet acceptance.

> After the meat was browned with onions,
> after the cup of sugar, Mother added in sour salt
> before simmering the meal stove-top for hours.

What I didn't learn from my parents or my own failed
marriage, you have mastered: love's work
takes opposites, sweet needing sour to grow a marriage.

> When the meat was tender, Mother
> thickened the sauce with ginger snaps.
> No one made a more savory brisket.

Just days ago, you hosted family and friends for a seder
on heirloom china. You served brisket and a recipe
for a loving marriage to pass down to your children.

Disrobing God

Shave off that shaggy beard.
You are no one's grandfather.

Remove the illusion
of white skin.

Admit the lie
that hides
beneath white robes.

Tell the truth.

You did not beget a son.
No one died for our sins.
No one prewrites the script
for our lives.

O we have created you,
fashioned from ego and hubris,
in our own image,
surrounded you with angels
waiting for us
beyond pearly gates.

Out of the wet tissues
of our need, out of the
sinking clay of our fears,
we whisper prayers in the ear
of a deaf universe.

I am not so foolish.

Redo your curriculum vitae.
Make up a different story.
One I can believe in.

Existential Questions

"Nothing is perfect," you said, settling
in a soft chair. The story I had been
telling myself about where we would go
from here evaporated like a whisper.

What do the tallied years tell us about
where we should go from here?
If knowing is comfort and too much
knowing a form of blindness,

where could we go from here now
that we know what we know?

To My Pain

Every day, you'd knock on my door,
enter with a big mouth and dirty shoes.
I am only a messenger, you'd explain,
a red alert climbing the stairs of my spine
to tell me, *Something is terribly wrong!*

I have consulted with physiatrists,
neuropathists, orthopedic surgeons.
Nothing can evict you, they claim,
or fix the cause; then they get busy
with scrips (oxycontin, percocet,
fentanyl patches) I refuse to fill.

Unlike pleasure, you go on and on,
persistent in your faithfulness.

Now that you have moved in,
now that we share a bed and sit across
from each other at the kitchen table,
now that whither I go you also go,
I will try to become a study in tolerance.

What else is there to do? Until death
do us part, we must learn to adjust
to living in the same house.

The Last Chapter

Here you are,
arrived
on the falling action,
helpless as a child
on a steep slide,
slipping
toward the dénouement
that promises
to untangle conflicts,
not a fairy tale's
happily-ever-after,
your final days
more like
the closing scene
of a Russian novel,
so that
at the ride's end,
as your feet
slam the dirt,
Death, that great resolver,
will open his arms to catch you.

Essence

The essence we are born with
walks with us
through all of our days.

If there is a soul, it is a coat
with turned-out pockets.

We are poor.
We are rich.
Everything we are
we spend.

Who hasn't felt
the bankruptcy
of a parched riverbed
waiting for spring's melt?

Always I have hungered
to make something
honest and beautiful
as rain.

Longing for the impossible
has stretched me
to near breaking,
and that is good.

Like a thrown-back fish
I wear the beards
of many hooks. Always
I wanted to be caught.
Always I wanted to be let loose.

Nature has taught me
that beauty and terror
need each other to survive.

How many times
I have climbed out
of my small self

to live in the eye
of a flower,
the maw of a gator.

At the bottom of everything sits loss.

All Your Days

All your days you have longed
for something you cannot name,
reached for something beyond your grasp,
hungered for something that didn't exist.

As time sped on, sped on, sped past,
you tried to hold on to what didn't last,
and now that your time is running out
you are no more than when you began,

and yet this life of going nowhere,
this life of a cistern that never filled,
you would not trade for purple robes,
you would not trade for riches or fame,

and never, not once in all your days,
did you stop loving this life you made.

Notes on the Represented Books

An Outward Track was published as the author's thesis for my Master of Arts in Humanities at Old Dominion University in 1980, available at Perry Library Special Collections (LD4331.H85G63).

Naming the Darkness, with an introduction by W. D. Snodgrass, was published by Road Publishers in 1991.

Light Persists won the Tampa Review Prize for Poetry and was published by the University of Tampa Press in 2006.

The Red Coat was published by FutureCycle Press in 2013.

In the Shadow of Paradise was published by FutureCycle Press in 2017.

Acknowledgments

Thanks to the editors of the following journals, in which the uncollected poems represented herein have previously appeared.

District/Lit: "To My Pain"
Lighthouse Point Magazine: "Black Skimmers Abecedarian"
Minerva Rising: "Existential Questions"
Southern Women's Review: "Because You Asked for a Happy Poem"
SWWIM: "Disrobing God"
Taj Mahal Review: "The Last Chapter"
The Jewish Writing Project: "A Savory Recipe"
Verdad: "Spring Cleaning"
Visions-International, the World Journal of Illustrated Poetry: "Essence,"
    "How to Make Friends with Wild Ducks"

"The Beauty of Abandonment" was the winner of the Goodreads Poetry Contest in May 2017 and appeared in its newsletter.

About FutureCycle Press

FutureCycle Press is dedicated to publishing lasting English-language poetry books, chapbooks, and anthologies in both print-on-demand and digital (ebook) formats. Founded in 2007 by long-time independent editor/publishers and partners Diane Kistner and Robert S. King, the press incorporated as a nonprofit in 2012. A number of our editors are distinguished poets and writers in their own right, and we have been actively involved in the small press movement going back to the early seventies.

The FutureCycle Poetry Book Prize and honorarium is awarded annually for the best full-length volume of poetry we publish in a calendar year. Introduced in 2013, our Good Works projects are anthologies devoted to issues of universal significance, with all proceeds donated to a related worthy cause. Our Selected Poems series highlights contemporary poets with a substantial body of work to their credit; with this series we strive to resurrect work that has had limited distribution and is now out of print.

We are dedicated to giving all of the authors we publish the care their work deserves, making our catalog of titles the most diverse and distinguished it can be, and paying forward any earnings to fund more great books.

We've learned a few things about independent publishing over the years. We've also evolved a unique, resilient publishing model that allows us to focus mainly on vetting and preserving for posterity the most books of exceptional quality without becoming overwhelmed with bookkeeping and mailing, fundraising activities, or taxing editorial and production "bubbles." To find out more about what we are doing, come see us at www.futurecycle.org.

The FutureCycle Poetry Book Prize

All full-length volumes of poetry published by FutureCycle Press in a given calendar year are considered for the annual FutureCycle Poetry Book Prize. This allows us to consider each submission on its own merits, outside of the context of a contest. Too, the judges see the finished book, which will have benefitted from the beautiful book design and strong editorial gloss we are famous for.

The book ranked the best in judging is announced as the prize-winner in the subsequent year. There is no fixed monetary award; instead, the winning poet receives an honorarium of 20% of the total net royalties from all poetry books and chapbooks the press sold online in the year the winning book was published. The winner is also accorded the honor of being on the panel of judges for the next year's competition; all judges receive copies of all contending books to keep for their personal library.

Made in the USA
Columbia, SC
18 July 2019